Parental Healing

Overcoming Childhood Trauma and Fostering Inner Strength

By

Marc K. Smith

Disclaimer

Table of Contents

Acknowledgements

Along the way to finishing "Parental Healing: Overcoming Childhood Trauma and Fostering Inner Strength," I have experienced tremendous development as a person and in my career. Without the kindness, wisdom, and belief of many extraordinary people, this adventure would never have happened.

To begin, I want to express my profound appreciation to the courageous individuals who have opened up about overcoming trauma in childhood. You have given others on similar journeys hope and crucial insights via your bravery and perseverance, which are the bedrock of this work.

Dr. Jane Thompson, whose ground-breaking work on childhood trauma laid the groundwork for this book, has my deepest gratitude. Her guidance and constant encouragement were crucial in helping me comprehend the intricacies of trauma and recovery.

My deepest gratitude goes go to Michael Clark, my editor, whose careful reading and insightful comments transformed my ideas into the book you see before you. All through the writing process, his skill and patience were priceless.

In addition, I want to thank the Parental Healing group for all their help. Your feedback, experiences, and shared wisdom were crucial in making this book as complete and sensitive as possible.

To my family, thank you for your endless love, patience, and belief in my work. Your encouragement made the tough moments of writing this book tolerable and the rewards all the more wonderful.

Finally, I thank you, the reader, for starting on this adventure with us. It is my earnest desire that the pages of this book provide you with understanding, solace, and a path toward healing and happiness.

Introduction

When I first went on the adventure of writing "Parental Healing: Overcoming Childhood Trauma and Fostering Inner Strength," I was painfully aware of the immense ocean of emotions and experiences I was about to travel. This book is not just a compilation of chapters and words; it is a heartfelt endeavor to reach out to people impacted by the shadows of childhood trauma and to pave a path toward healing and inner strength.

The genesis of this book lies in the intricate and sometimes hidden struggles that I have encountered in my years as a therapist. Time and again, I have sat across individuals who, despite various backgrounds, shared a common thread - the deep and lasting impact of their early experiences. These interactions, both powerful and humbling, have taught me that the journey of recovery is as unique as the one undertaking it. Yet, some universal truths and tactics might lead us on this path.

"Parental Healing" is an invitation to go on a path of self-discovery and healing. It is written for persons who have experienced childhood trauma and for others who seek to understand and help them. This book is also an homage to the resilience of the human spirit and the remarkable power we have to transform grief into strength.

Each chapter of this book is designed to offer insight, comfort, and practical assistance. The stories recounted are authentic, culled from the lives of individuals who have graciously opened their hearts to aid others. These narratives are not just tales of grief and suffering; they are beacons of hope and resilience. They demonstrate that while pain can leave profound scars, it is possible to heal, grow, and find joy again.

As you turn these pages, you will find a blend of professional insights, personal observations, and therapeutic practices. The book begins by addressing the nature of childhood trauma - its forms, its repercussions, and its subtle methods of molding our adult lives. It is vital to acknowledge and comprehend trauma to begin the healing process. From there, we dig into the first steps of recovery, highlighting the power of acknowledgment, acceptance, and getting help.

Vulnerability, often perceived as a weakness, is reimagined in this book as a cornerstone of healing. You will learn about the transforming power of opening up and accepting vulnerability, not as a liability but as a gateway to deeper self-understanding and connection with others.

The heart of the book resides in the stories of resilience - stories of individuals who have walked through the dark valleys of their history and emerged stronger. These anecdotes are not only uplifting but also instructional, offering essential insights on coping, healing, and flourishing.

Building inner strength is a significant theme of this book. You will discover tools and practices to promote emotional resilience and a good self-image. The function of relationships in recovery is also discussed, underlining the need to nurture good ties and set limits.

One of the most significant components of this trip is the cultivation of happiness. This book provides practical guidance on attaining joy and fulfillment, even after experiencing tragedy. It underlines the idea that happiness is not only a destination but a daily practice, a choice we make among our circumstances.

The final chapters focus on breaking the cycle of trauma and being a source of strength for the next generation. This book highlights the obligation and chance to steer children towards a healthier, more nurturing environment, free from the shadows of our past traumas.

As you embark on this path with "Parental Healing," realize that healing is not a linear process. It is a route filled with ups and downs, wins and losses. But with each step, you get closer to a place of understanding, serenity, and joy. This book is both a guide and a companion, offering you the tools and support you need to traverse the intricacies of recovering from childhood trauma.

In closing, I send my heartfelt gratitude to you, the reader. By choosing to engage with this book, you are taking a brave and major step towards healing and progress. Whether you are personally affected by childhood trauma or are assisting someone who is, know that this road, though tough, is immensely rewarding. May the pages of "Parental Healing" provide you insights, solace, and the confidence to accept your journey towards a life of strength, happiness, and inner peace.

Chapter 1: Understanding Childhood Trauma

Defining Childhood Trauma

Childhood trauma is a complicated and varied issue that impacts individuals across many phases of their lives. It is crucial to understand and characterize it precisely to address its tremendous impacts on the emotional, psychological, and physical well-being of people touched.

1. What is Childhood Trauma?

Childhood trauma refers to a child's experience of an incident or set of events that are emotionally painful or distressful, which typically results in enduring mental and physical damage. Trauma can arise from one-time occurrences or continual, persistent stress, and its impact can vary greatly depending on the individual's age, environment, and ability to cope.

2. Types of Childhood Trauma

- **Physical Abuse:** Involving physical abuse or injury to the child.
- **Emotional Abuse:** Involving verbal abuse, emotional manipulation, or extreme disregard of a child's emotional needs.
- **Sexual Abuse:** Involving any coerced or manipulative sexual connection.
- **Neglect:** Failing to provide for the child's basic needs, especially emotional nurturing.
- **Witnessing Violence or Severe Discord:** Experiencing or observing violence in the household or community.
- **Sudden Loss or Separation:** Experiencing the sudden loss of or separation from a loved one.
- **Natural Disasters or Accidents:** Enduring catastrophic disasters like

earthquakes, floods, or serious accidents.

3. The Impact of Childhood Trauma

The impacts of childhood trauma can be deep and long-lasting, influencing an individual's health and behavior years after the traumatic incident has occurred. Some of the common impacts include:

- **Emotional Issues:** Anxiety, depression, fear, and feelings of isolation.
- **Behavioral Changes:** Aggression, self-harm, or substance misuse.
- **Cognitive Effects:** Difficulties with concentration, memory, and problem-solving.
- **Physical Health Problems:** Increased risk of health conditions like heart disease, obesity, and diabetes.

4. Recognizing Symptoms of Childhood Trauma

Children may not always be able to verbalize their feelings or may try to hide their distress. Some symptoms that a youngster may have undergone trauma include:

- Sudden shifts in behavior or mood.
- Regression to earlier developmental stages.
- Withdrawal from friends or customary hobbies.
- Physical symptoms without a clear reason.

5. Importance of Early Intervention

Identifying and resolving childhood trauma early can dramatically lessen the long-term impact on an individual's life. Early intervention options can involve treatment, assistance from loved ones, and building a stable, supportive environment.

6. Resilience and Recovery

While childhood trauma can have enduring impacts, individuals also have a tremendous ability for resilience and rehabilitation. With the correct help and tools, many people who have survived trauma may enjoy healthy, productive lives. Building resilience entails building a supportive group, learning coping techniques, and obtaining professional help when necessary.

Defining childhood trauma is not just about recognizing the types of traumatic events and their possible repercussions. It's about recognizing the substantial and sometimes hidden problems that many persons confront and making proactive efforts to support healing and recovery. By understanding and addressing childhood trauma, we may assist individuals and communities in moving toward a more hopeful and resilient future.

The Long-term Effects of Trauma on Individuals

Understanding the long-term repercussions of trauma is vital in acknowledging its significant and permanent influence on individuals. Trauma, especially when encountered throughout childhood, can leave a permanent effect on a person's emotional, psychological, and physical well-being. This section dives into the numerous dimensions of these long-term impacts.

1. Emotional and Psychological Effects

- **Mental Health Disorders:** Trauma can raise the chance of developing mental health disorders such as post-traumatic stress disorder (PTSD), depression, anxiety, and mood disorders.
- **Emotional Dysregulation:** Individuals may struggle with controlling emotions, leading to

powerful and unpredictable emotional responses.

- **Impaired Self-Esteem:** Trauma can lead to emotions of worthlessness, humiliation, and a skewed self-image.
- **Difficulty in Trust and Relationships:** Trauma survivors may find it hard to trust others or build healthy relationships due to fear of betrayal or abandonment.

2. Behavioral Consequences

- **Avoidance and Isolation:** Many persons may avoid people, places, or events that remind them of the trauma, resulting in social isolation.
- **Risky activities:** Some may engage in risky or self-destructive activities, such as substance abuse or self-harm, as a coping method.
- **Relationship Challenges:** Issues such as intimacy problems, difficulty in establishing stable partnerships, or

repeating destructive relationship patterns are frequent.

3. Cognitive and Developmental Impacts

- **Learning and remembering Problems:** Trauma can disrupt cognitive skills, resulting in issues in concentration, decision-making, and remembering.
- **Developmental Delays:** In children, trauma can result in delays in developmental milestones or return to earlier developmental stages.
- **Altered Worldview:** Trauma can lead to a chronic sense of risk and a negative viewpoint on the world, altering life choices and prospects.

4. Physical Health Effects

- **Chronic Health diseases:** Trauma is linked to chronic health diseases like heart disease, obesity, diabetes, and gastrointestinal disorders.

- **Somatic Symptoms:** Trauma survivors may endure bodily symptoms without a medical explanation, such as chronic pain or exhaustion.
- **Impact on Brain Development:** In children, continuous exposure to trauma can influence brain development, potentially leading to long-term abnormalities in brain structure and function.

5. Societal and Economic Impacts

- **Workplace Challenges:** Trauma can hinder job performance and career growth owing to difficulty in attention, absenteeism, or interpersonal disputes.
- **Economic hardship:** The cost of healthcare for physical and mental health concerns associated with trauma can lead to financial hardship.
- **Social Interactions:** Trauma survivors might struggle with social

norms and interactions, leading to challenges in community engagement.

6. Intergenerational Trauma

- **Transmission to Next Generation:** The impact of trauma can transcend generations, as parents may unintentionally pass on patterns of behavior and emotional responses to their offspring.

7. Coping and Resilience

While the long-term impacts of trauma can be devastating, it is crucial to underline the possibilities for resilience and rehabilitation. With sufficient assistance, treatment, and coping strategies, many individuals learn to manage the effects of trauma and lead productive lives. Recognizing the indicators and seeking timely care are critical aspects of this healing process.

In summary, the long-term repercussions of trauma are wide-ranging, including emotional and psychological health, behavior, cognition, physical health, and societal engagement. Understanding these repercussions is vital for offering appropriate assistance and treatments to help persons heal and reclaim their lives.

Chapter 2: The First Steps to Healing

Acknowledging and Accepting the Past

"Acknowledging and Accepting the Past" is a vital stage in the road of healing from trauma. This process entails understanding the impact of traumatic experiences and accepting them as a part of one's history, which is crucial for moving forward. It is a tough yet crucial step in overcoming the impacts of trauma and developing a foundation for a better, more resilient future.

1. Understanding the Need for Acknowledgment

- **Recognition of Trauma:** The first stage is to accept that a traumatic incident or set of events occurred and that they have had a substantial impact on one's life. This awareness is vital in validating one's feelings and experiences.

- **Breaking the Silence:** Many persons who have experienced trauma may have kept silent about their experiences. Speaking about the trauma or writing it down can be a vital step in admitting its reality.

2. The Role of Acceptance

- **Accepting Reality:** Acceptance involves coming to grips with what happened, without necessarily condoning or agreeing with it. It's about recognizing that the past cannot be changed, but one's response to it can.

- **Separating Past from Present:** By accepting the past, individuals can start to distinguish their former experiences from their current existence, diminishing the hold that painful memories have on their present.

3. Challenges in Acknowledgment and Acceptance

- **Emotional Pain:** Confronting traumatic situations can be emotionally unpleasant and may bring up feelings of wrath, despair, or grief. It's crucial to approach this procedure calmly and with assistance.
- **Denial and Avoidance:** Some may find it simpler to reject the impact of trauma or avoid dealing with it. Recognizing these protective mechanisms is a step towards conquering them.

4. Strategies for Acknowledgment and Acceptance

- **Therapy:** Professional aid such as therapy can provide a safe and supportive environment for acknowledging and processing trauma.

- **Mindfulness and Self-Compassion:** Practices like mindfulness can aid in being present and cultivating self-compassion, making it easier to tolerate uncomfortable emotions and memories.
- **Journaling:** Writing about one's experiences can be a therapeutic technique to acknowledge and accept the past.
- **Support Groups:** Sharing experiences with people who have gone through similar situations can be validating and aid in the process of acceptance.

5. Moving Beyond the Past

- **Empowerment:** Acknowledging and accepting the past can be powerful, as it empowers individuals to take control of their healing process.

- **Groundwork for Healing:** This process establishes the groundwork for later healing work, such as addressing present emotional and behavioral patterns caused by past trauma.

6. Continuing the Journey

- **Ongoing Process:** Acknowledgment and acceptance are not one-time events but an ongoing process that may need to be repeated as one advances through different phases of healing.
- **Seeking Ongoing Support:** It's crucial to continue seeking support and adopting coping skills, especially during hard times.

In conclusion, admitting and embracing the past are key steps in healing from trauma. They involve recognizing the reality of the trauma, understanding its consequences, and accepting it as part of one's life story. While tough, this process is crucial for breaking free from the grip of the past and moving toward a future of resilience and emotional well-being.

Seeking Professional Help

"Seeking Professional Help" is a critical chapter on the road to recovering from childhood trauma. It emphasizes the significance of reaching out to specialists for help, support, and therapy, and gives a path for navigating this critical step.

1. Understanding the Importance of Professional Help

- **Competence in Trauma:** Trained experts possess the competence to comprehend and treat the multifaceted repercussions of trauma.
- **Secure Space:** Therapy provides a secure and confidential setting to address sensitive subjects.
- **Personalized Care:** Professionals can tailor their approach to meet individual requirements and situations.

2. Types of Professional Help Available

- **Psychologists and Psychiatrists:** They offer therapy and, in the case of psychiatrists, can also prescribe medication.
- **Licensed Clinical Social Workers and Counselors:** These professionals provide counseling and support services.
- **Specialists in Trauma Therapy:** Therapists who specialize in trauma can offer specific therapies like EMDR (Eye Movement Desensitization and Reprocessing) or trauma-focused CBT (Cognitive Behavioral Therapy).

3. Overcoming Barriers to Seeking Help

- **Stigma:** Understanding that getting treatment is a show of strength, not weakness, can help overcome cultural stigma.
- **Financial Concerns:** Exploring sliding scale prices, insurance

alternatives, or community resources can make therapy more accessible.

- **Fear and Mistrust:** Building trust takes time, but a professional's help can be invaluable in the healing journey.

4. Finding the Right Professional

- **references:** Getting references from healthcare practitioners, trusted persons, or support groups might be a good start.
- **Research:** Researching therapists' qualifications, areas of specialization, and therapeutic methodologies is vital.
- **Consultation:** Many therapists offer initial appointments to establish fit and comfort levels.

5. Preparing for Therapy

- **Setting Goals:** Understanding what you want to achieve from treatment can influence the approach.
- **Openness:** Being open to the process, especially when it feels tough, is vital for progress.
- **Consistency:** Regular attendance and engagement are crucial to the effectiveness of therapy.

6. The Role of Medication

- **Consideration as a Tool:** Medication can be a valuable tool in treating symptoms, but it's often most effective when accompanied by therapy.
- **Expert advice:** Decisions about medication should always be made under the direction of a skilled expert.

7. Integrating Therapy into the Healing Journey

- **Part of a Holistic Approach:** Therapy is one component of a holistic approach to healing from trauma.
- **Long-Term Perspective:** Healing is a long-term process, and therapy can be altered over time to fit developing requirements.

8. Embracing the Journey with Professional Support

- **Empowerment Through Treatment:** Engaging in treatment can be empowering, providing skills and insights to manage life more effectively.
- **establishing Resilience:** Professional help can aid in establishing resilience and coping methods for the future.

Seeking professional therapy is a key step in the healing journey from childhood trauma. It entails acknowledging the need for expert counsel, overcoming barriers to getting help, and engaging actively in the therapeutic process. By doing so, individuals open up a road to greater understanding, effective coping skills, and a more resilient self, building the framework for a happier and more rewarding future.

Chapter 3: Embracing Vulnerability

Learning to Open Up

"Learning to Open Up" is a vital stage in the road to healing from childhood trauma. This process entails breaking down the walls that hinder individuals from communicating their feelings and experiences, which is vital for emotional healing and creating good relationships.

1. Understanding the Importance of Opening Up

- **Emotional Release:** Expressing feelings is crucial for emotional well-being. Bottled-up sentiments can lead to increased stress, worry, and despair.

- **Building ties:** Sharing your story can enhance your ties with others and help you feel less alienated.
- **Facilitating Healing:** Talking about trauma can be helpful and is often a vital element of the healing process.

2. Overcoming the Fear of Vulnerability

- **Changing Perspective:** Understand that vulnerability is not a weakness, but a power that allows for meaningful connections and healing.
- **Simple Steps:** Start by sharing simple, less scary things and progressively build up to more substantial issues.
- **Safe place:** Choose a safe and supportive place or person to begin opening up to.

3. Developing Trust

- **Choosing the Right People:** Share your thoughts and feelings with people who have proven themselves to be trustworthy and supportive.

- **Listening to Intuition:** Trust your intuition regarding when and with whom to share your experiences.
- **Understanding Boundaries:** Recognize that it's fair to set boundaries regarding how much you share and with whom.

4. Communicating Effectively

- **Clarity in Expression:** Learn to express your thoughts and feelings clearly and directly.
- **Non-Verbal Communication:** Be aware of and employ non-verbal communication strategies, such as eye contact and body language.
- **Active Listening:** Practice active listening when people are sharing with you, creating a reciprocal and helpful discourse.

5. Utilizing Supportive Tools

- **Journaling:** Writing can be a means to articulate ideas and emotions before verbalizing them.
- **Therapy:** A therapist can provide a safe area to explore and practice opening up.
- **Support Groups:** Sharing experiences with others who have similar tales can be less daunting and incredibly validating.

6. Embracing the Challenges

- **Acknowledging Discomfort:** Recognize that feeling uncomfortable is a natural part of the process and doesn't imply you should stop.
- **Patience with Yourself:** Understand that this is a talent that requires time to master. Be patient with yourself.

7. The Power of Reciprocity

- **Engaging in Mutual Sharing:** Relationships are built on give and take. Be open to listening to others as much as you share with them.

- **Creating a Supportive Network:** Through reciprocal sharing, you can create a network of support and understanding.

8. Nurturing Self-Compassion

- **Self-Understanding:** Be kind to yourself as you traverse the complexities of your emotions and experiences.
- **Self-Care:** Engage in self-care techniques that enhance your emotional strength and resilience.

Learning to open up is a vital element of healing from trauma. It entails appreciating the significance of sharing your story, overcoming anxieties of vulnerability, creating trust, communicating effectively, and being compassionate with yourself. As you learn to communicate your thoughts and feelings, you will find greater emotional release, deeper connections, and important strides in your road toward healing and wholeness.

The Power of Vulnerability in Healing

"The Power of Vulnerability in Healing" is an essential chapter for anyone walking the hard path of recovery from childhood trauma. This episode underlines the transforming impact that embracing vulnerability may play in the healing process.

1. Redefining Vulnerability

- **Strength, Not Weakness:** Vulnerability is sometimes mistaken as weakness, yet in the context of healing, it is a tremendous strength. It involves the bravery to face one's feelings and experiences freely.
- **Gateway to Authenticity:** Being vulnerable helps individuals to show their actual selves, creating authenticity in their personal growth and relationships.

2. Vulnerability and Emotional Healing

- **Processing Trauma:** Vulnerability is crucial to processing traumatic events. It entails acknowledging and expressing sentiments that might have been suppressed.
- **Building Emotional Resilience:** By encountering tough emotions, individuals develop stronger resilience, learning to manage and respond to emotional difficulties more successfully.

3. Vulnerability in Therapy

- **Therapeutic Relationship:** A therapeutic context typically needs vulnerability. Opening up to a therapist can lead to more effective treatment outcomes.
- **Safe area for Exploration:** Therapy gives a safe area where individuals can explore their weaknesses without judgment.

4. Vulnerability and Relationships

- **Deepening relationships:** Vulnerability provides for deeper emotional relationships with people, as it fosters openness and mutual understanding.
- **Trust and Support:** Sharing one's inner concerns, challenges, and hopes can create trust and establish a strong support network.

5. Challenges in Embracing Vulnerability

- **Overcoming Fear:** The fear of being judged, rejected, or injured can make vulnerability hard. It takes time to overcome this fear.
- **Cultural and Societal Norms:** Societal standards often inhibit vulnerability, especially in specific cultures or communities, making it tougher to embrace.

6. Steps to Embrace Vulnerability

- **Self-awareness:** Begin with self-reflection to understand your anxieties and hesitations about being vulnerable.

- **Start modest:** Practice vulnerability in modest, attainable increments. Share something minor with a trusted individual and gradually expand from there.

- **Mindfulness Practices:** Techniques like mindfulness can aid in remaining present and minimizing anxiety about vulnerability.

7. The Role of Self-Compassion

- **Kindness to Self:** Be gentle to yourself as you negotiate the hurdles of being vulnerable. Recognize that setbacks are part of the process.

- **Understanding Personal Limits:** It's crucial to know your limits and set boundaries around vulnerability. It's a personal journey, and everyone's capacity varies.

8. The Transformative Impact of Vulnerability

- **Personal Growth:** Embracing vulnerability can lead to considerable personal growth, self-acceptance, and a better understanding of oneself.
- **Empowerment:** There is an empowering component to vulnerability — it takes back control from past traumas and rewrites the story on one's terms.

The power of vulnerability in healing is profound and diverse. It functions as a catalyst for emotional processing, strengthening resilience, deepening connections, and stimulating personal growth. Embracing vulnerability is a brave and necessary step on the road to healing from childhood trauma, leading to a more authentic, resilient, and satisfied self.

Chapter 4: Stories of Resilience

John's Journey: Overcoming Neglect

John's story is a striking monument to the human spirit's capacity for resilience and transformation. His tale of overcoming mistreatment and discovering his road to recovery and self-discovery offers hope and inspiration to others facing similar circumstances.

1. The Shadow of Neglect

John grew up in a family where emotional and physical maltreatment was widespread. His parents, distracted by their troubles, often left John to fend for himself, unable to offer the basic emotional support and direction a youngster requires. This neglect left John feeling alienated, unworthy, and invisible.

2. The Impact of Neglect

As he grew older, the repercussions of this neglect became more obvious. John battled with low self-esteem, trouble developing connections, and a deep-seated sense of insecurity. He found it hard to trust others, always dreading desertion or rejection.

3. The Turning Point

John's turning moment came in his late twenties when a key relationship ended, pushing him into a period of introspection. It was during this time that he understood the extent to which his childhood experiences were impacting his adult life. This discovery marked the beginning of his therapeutic path.

4. Seeking Help

John made the daring step of seeking professional treatment. He started therapy, where he began the process of unraveling the layers of his childhood neglect. In therapy, he learned to understand and explain his feelings, something he had never been taught to do as a youngster.

5. Learning to Self-Parent

A key aspect of John's therapy was learning how to 'self-parent.' He worked on giving himself the love, attention, and care he didn't receive as a youngster. This includes developing routines, engaging in self-care techniques, and nurturing his interests and passions.

6. Building Relationships

One of the toughest elements for John was learning to create and maintain healthy connections. He had to learn to trust others and recognize that not everyone would mimic the maltreatment he experienced in his youth. He slowly started to build significant connections, both platonically and romantically.

7. Embracing Vulnerability

John learned the power of vulnerability. By opening up about his experiences and allowing himself to be seen, he found strength and connection. He attended support groups where he told his tale and listened to others, learning he was not alone in his experiences.

8. Discovering Inner Strength

Through his trip, John discovered an inner power he didn't realize he had. Each step towards healing reinforced his tenacity and ability to withstand adversity. He learned to regard his past not as a source of shame but as a monument to his strength.

9. Giving Back

John's experience inspired him to help others. He became an advocate for child welfare, participating with groups that protect neglected children. This work gave him a feeling of purpose and allowed him to heal further.

10. Continuing the Journey

John recognizes that healing is a constant process. He continues to attend therapy, participate in self-care activities, and cultivate his connections. His journey is a continuous movement toward self-discovery, acceptance, and growth.

John's experience is a compelling reminder that overcoming neglect is possible. It involves courage, support, and a dedication to self-healing. John's experience shows that, despite a tough start in life, individuals can discover strength, create meaningful connections, and lead a rewarding life. His journey is an cncouragement to those who have suffered similar hardships, bringing hope and a route to healing.

Maria's Tale: Surviving Emotional Abuse

Maria's tale is a tragic example of the tenacity of the human spirit in the face of emotional assault. Her journey from the pain of abuse to a life of empowerment and self-compassion shows a road of recovery for others who have endured similar tragedies.

1. The Reality of Emotional Abuse

Maria grew raised in a home where emotional abuse was the norm. Her parents, often critical and emotionally manipulative, used words and emotional neglect as weapons. This setting left Maria feeling useless, insecure, and continuously yearning for unattainable approval.

2. Recognizing the Abuse

For years, Maria normalized her family's behavior, not recognizing it as abuse. It was not until her college years, via encounters with friends and lecturers, that she began to see the oddity of her upbringing. This discovery was both startling and freeing.

3. The Courage to Seek Help

Acknowledging her trauma drove Maria to seek professional therapy. She started treatment, where she learned to understand and verbalize the emotional trauma she had undergone. Therapy gave them a secure area to analyze and process her complex feelings.

4. Breaking the Cycle

One of Maria's main concerns was stopping the cycle of abuse. She had internalized many of the bad lessons from her past, which harmed her self-esteem and relationships. Through treatment, she learned to challenge these negative beliefs and establish a more positive self-image.

5. Building Self-Compassion

A significant component of Maria's rehabilitation was cultivating self-compassion. She learned to treat herself with the care and understanding she had always hoped for from her family. This entailed nourishing her needs, setting appropriate boundaries, and engaging in self-care routines.

6. Developing Healthy Relationships

Maria struggled with trust and intimacy owing to her past of emotional abuse. She had to learn how to build and sustain good relationships. This includes understanding what a good relationship looks like and how to communicate effectively and assertively.

7. Finding Empowerment in Vulnerability

Sharing her story was a crucial step for Maria. She found power in vulnerability, realizing that her voice and experiences mattered. This not only assisted her healing but also linked her with others who had similar situations.

8. Advocacy and Helping Others

As Maria healed, she became passionate about helping others who had undergone emotional abuse. She became active in advocacy work, sharing her story to raise awareness and provide assistance to others in similar situations.

9. Embracing Life Beyond Abuse

Maria learned to embrace life beyond her past. She explored her interests, acquired rewarding hobbies, and built a life that mirrored her values and ambitions, free from the shadow of her past.

10. A Continuous Journey

Maria recognizes that healing from emotional abuse is an ongoing process. She continues to engage in therapy, maintain her support networks, and practice self-compassion. Her journey is one of ongoing growth and self-discovery.

Maria's account of surviving emotional abuse is a story of overcoming, tenacity, and hope. Her narrative illustrates the significance of detecting abuse, seeking help, changing the cycle, and finding empowerment in one's voice. Maria's experiences serve as a light of hope for others, proving that it is possible to go beyond a traumatic past and build a life of self-worth, love, and contentment.

Alex's Road to Recovery: Healing from Physical Abuse

Alex's journey is a dramatic account of overcoming the wounds of physical abuse and finding a road to healing and strength. His narrative serves as an encouraging monument to the courage and resilience available in the face of hardship.

1. The Reality of Physical Abuse

Alex grew raised in a home where physical abuse was a frequent occurrence. The persistent terror and physical harm inflicted by a family member left severe emotional and physical scars. This abuse led to feelings of powerlessness, anxiety, and a deep-seated sense of worthlessness.

2. Acknowledging the Abuse

For a long time, Alex battled to admit the abuse. He was engulfed in a mix of denial, shame, and guilt. It was only after a serious event that led to hospitalization that Alex began to accept the truth of his circumstances and see the need for change.

3. The First Steps Toward Healing

Deciding to break the pattern of abuse, Alex sought treatment. He reached out to a psychotherapist skilled in dealing with physical abuse survivors. This move marked the beginning of his healing path, allowing him a secure space to process his experiences.

4. Overcoming Physical and Emotional Scars

In therapy, Alex worked with both the physical and emotional implications of his trauma. He acquired coping methods to deal with the anxiety and flashbacks and worked on regaining his self-esteem and feeling of self-worth.

5. The Role of Physical Activity

A key component of Alex's recuperation was physical activity. Engaging in sports and exercise not only helped him recover his physical strength but also gave him a mental outlet, helping him to channel his emotions constructively.

6. Building a Support Network

Alex learned the necessity of a support network. He progressively opened up to friends and joined support groups where he connected with others who had similar experiences. These ties gave empathy, understanding, and encouragement.

7. Learning to Trust Again

One of Alex's toughest struggles was learning to trust people again. Through treatment and pleasant experiences, he gradually learned that not everyone would cause him harm and that he could create healthy and supportive relationships.

8. Reclaiming Control of His Life

Part of Alex's rehabilitation was recovering control over his life. He made conscious decisions about his relationships, job, and how he spent his time, moving away from the victim mindset that had been imposed on him by his abuser.

9. Giving Voice to His Experiences

As he healed, Alex found strength in sharing his tale. He became involved in advocacy and awareness initiatives for physical abuse survivors, using his experiences to aid others.

10. A Journey of Ongoing Recovery

Alex recognizes that healing is a continual process. He continues to attend therapy sessions, is active in support groups, and maintains a healthy lifestyle. He regards each day as a step forward in his journey towards a more serene and meaningful life.

Alex's road to rehabilitation from physical assault is a narrative of strength, endurance, and hope. His narrative highlights the necessity of identifying abuse, obtaining professional help, developing a support network, and finding empowerment in one's experiences. Alex's story offers inspiration and hope to others who may be facing similar circumstances, proving that it is possible to overcome abuse and lead a life distinguished by courage and healing.

Chapter 5: Building Inner Strength

Techniques for Emotional Resilience

Emotional resilience refers to the ability to adapt to stressful conditions, crises, or trauma. It's not about avoiding pain or fear, but rather learning how to absorb and recover from these experiences. Developing emotional resilience is vital for navigating life's challenges efficiently. Here are some major techniques:

1. Self-Awareness

- **Understanding Emotions:** Recognize and comprehend your emotions. Identify what provokes tension or bad feelings and how you generally respond.

- **Mindfulness Practices:** Engage in mindfulness meditation to develop awareness of your thoughts and feelings without judgment.

2. Positive Thinking

- **Reframe Negative thinking:** Challenge and replace negative thinking with more positive, realistic ones.
- **Focus on the Good:** Cultivate a habit of identifying and appreciating the positive aspects of your life, especially in difficult circumstances.

3. Emotional Regulation

- **Stress Management Strategies:** Learn stress-reduction strategies such as deep breathing, gradual muscle relaxation, or visualization.
- **Stay Calm Under Pressure:** Practice staying calm and composed in tough

situations, using your stress management strategies.

4. Building Connections

- **Nurture ties:** Maintain healthy, supportive ties with family and friends. Social support is crucial in resiliency.
- **Community Involvement:** Participate in community groups or activities where you can connect with others.

5. Healthy Boundaries

- **Set Limits:** Learn to say no and set healthy boundaries in your personal and professional life.
- **Balance Giving and Receiving:** Make sure you are not overextending yourself in helping others at the price of your well-being.

6. Problem-Solving Skills

- **Develop Problem-Solving Strategies:** Enhance your ability to spot problems and develop realistic solutions.
- **Flexibility:** Be open to altering your strategies if the initial answers don't work.

7. Self-Care

- **Regular Physical Activity:** Engage in physical activities that you enjoy. Exercise is a powerful stress reducer.
- **Balanced Diet and Sleep:** Ensure a balanced diet and appropriate sleep, as physical health substantially impacts emotional resilience.

8. Seeking Help When Needed

- **Professional Support:** Don't hesitate to seek professional help if you're struggling to cope. Therapists can provide techniques and help in increasing resilience.

- **Support Groups:** Consider joining support groups where you may share experiences and learn from others.

9. Continuous Learning and Growth

- **Learn from Experiences:** View problems as chances for progress. Reflect on what you've learned from past events.
- **Stay Curious:** Cultivate an attitude of curiosity and a desire to learn new things, which can boost your flexibility and resilience.

10. Practicing Gratitude

- **Gratitude Journaling:** Keep a gratitude notebook to remind yourself of the great things in your life.
- **Expressing thanks:** Regularly express thanks to others, which helps boost mood and emotional well-being.

Building emotional resilience is a dynamic and continuing process. It requires establishing a deep understanding of oneself, nurturing meaningful connections, maintaining physical and mental health, and acquiring efficient coping strategies. By applying these skills to daily life, individuals can strengthen their capacity to navigate through life's problems with strength and grace.

Fostering a Positive Self-Image

Developing a positive self-image is vital for general well-being and happiness. It entails establishing a perception of oneself that is grounded in realism, acceptance, and self-compassion. Here are key techniques to build a positive self-image:

1. Practice Self-Acceptance

- **Acknowledge Your Worth:** Recognize and affirm your innate worth as a person, independent of achievements or external validation.
- **Embrace Your Uniqueness:** Celebrate your distinct qualities and characteristics. Understand that everyone has strengths and weaknesses.

2. Challenge Negative Self-Talk

- **Identify Negative Patterns:** Become aware of negative ideas and attitudes about yourself.
- **Reframe thinking:** Replace critical or negative thinking with more positive, realistic ones. Practice conversing with yourself as you would with a close friend.

3. Set Realistic Goals

- **Achievable Objectives:** Set goals that are demanding yet achievable. Accomplishing these goals might increase your sense of efficacy and self-esteem.
- **appreciate Successes:** Recognize and appreciate your achievements, no matter how minor.

4. Engage in Positive Activities

- **Pursue Interests:** Engage in things that you enjoy and that make you feel good about yourself.

- **Develop talents:** Invest time in learning new talents or hobbies. This boosts your sense of accomplishment and self-worth.

5. Cultivate a Healthy Lifestyle

- **Physical Activity:** Regular exercise can boost mood and self-image.
- **Balanced Diet:** Eating a healthy diet helps to a better sense of self.
- **Adequate Rest:** Ensure you receive enough sleep, as it influences your mood and self-perception.

6. Surround Yourself with Positive Influences

- **Supportive ties:** Build ties with people that encourage and support you.
- **Limit Negative Influences:** Distance yourself from settings or individuals who damage your self-esteem.

7. Practice Self-Compassion

- **Kindness to Self:** Treat yourself with kindness and empathy, especially during difficult circumstances.
- **Forgive Yourself:** Learn to forgive yourself for previous faults. Understand that making mistakes is a part of being human.

8. Reflect on Your Strengths and Achievements

- **Strengths Inventory:** Regularly reflect on your strengths and positive attributes.
- **Accomplishments Review:** Remind yourself of your triumphs and how you overcame past problems.

9. Seek Feedback Constructively

- **Openness to input:** Be open to constructive input and use it as a chance for improvement.

- **Discernment:** Learn to discriminate between beneficial feedback and criticism that is not constructive.

10. Utilize Affirmations and Visualization

- **Positive Affirmations:** Use affirmations to encourage positive attitudes about yourself.
- **Visualization Techniques:** Visualize yourself attaining your goals and being the person you wish to be.

Fostering a healthy self-image is a process that involves self-awareness, self-care, and active engagement in actions that increase your impression of oneself. By applying these tactics, you can build a more positive, realistic, and compassionate image of oneself, which is a cornerstone for a fulfilling and resilient existence.

Chapter 6: The Role of Relationships in Healing

Nurturing Healthy Relationships

Nurturing good connections is vital for emotional well-being and personal progress. Mutual respect, trust, and communication are the foundations of healthy relationships. Here are some techniques to build and maintain such relationships:

1. Effective Communication

- **Open and Honest Dialogue:** Encourage open and honest communication. Share your opinions and feelings clearly and listen actively to others.
- **Conflict Resolution:** Learn to confront problems effectively,

without resorting to blame or avoidance.

2. Building Trust

- **Consistency and Reliability:** Be consistent and reliable in your activities and commitments. This creates trust over time.
- **Transparency:** Be transparent in your goals and behavior. Honesty develops deeper trust and understanding.

3. Showing Respect

- **Valuing Opinions:** Show respect for others' opinions and feelings, even when they differ from your own.
- **Acknowledging Boundaries:** Respect personal boundaries. Understanding and accepting each other's limits is crucial to a good partnership.

4. Expressing Appreciation

- **Regular Affirmation:** Regularly express appreciation and thanks for the individuals in your life. This encourages favorable relationship dynamics.
- **Recognizing Efforts:** Acknowledge the efforts and contributions of others. Everyone desires to be respected and acknowledged.

5. Practicing Empathy

- **Understanding Perspectives:** Try to understand things from the other person's perspective. This deepens emotional ties.
- **Being Supportive:** Offer support and empathy during hard situations. A little empathy goes a long way in strengthening friendships.

6. Balancing Independence and Togetherness

- **Personal Space:** Maintain your individuality and respect others' desire for personal space. Healthy partnerships give opportunities for personal growth.
- **Shared Activities:** Engage in activities together that create intimacy and shared experiences.

7. Maintaining a Positive Attitude

- **Optimism:** Approach your relationships with optimism. An optimistic viewpoint can influence the overall tone of encounters.
- **Resilience:** Be resilient in the face of interpersonal challenges. Work together to tackle obstacles.

8. Seeking and Offering Help

- **Mutual Support:** Be open to seeking and offering support when needed. Reciprocity strengthens the bond.

- **Professional Help:** If needed, don't hesitate to seek professional guidance, including couples or family therapy.

9. Cultivating Shared Goals and Values

- **Common Objectives:** Develop shared aims and values. This gives a sense of unity and direction in the connection.
- **Regular Check-ins:** Have regular discussions about your goals, aspirations, and values to guarantee alignment and mutual understanding.

10. Celebrating and Enjoying Each Other

- **Quality Time:** Spend quality time together. This develops intimacy and delight in the partnership.
- **Acknowledging Milestones:** Celebrate major milestones and successes together.

Nurturing healthy relationships needs effort, commitment, and a willingness to grow together. By practicing good communication, creating trust, showing respect and appreciation, and keeping a balance between independence and togetherness, you can cultivate deep and fulfilling relationships. Remember, strong relationships are not devoid of obstacles, but they are distinguished by the capacity to handle these challenges together helpfully and constructively.

Setting Boundaries

Setting boundaries is a vital component of maintaining successful relationships and personal well-being. It requires understanding and respecting your limits and conveying them effectively to others. Here's a guide on setting and maintaining effective boundaries:

1. Understanding Boundaries

- **Personal Limits:** Recognize your emotional, mental, physical, and spiritual limits. Understand what you can tolerate and accept and what makes you feel uncomfortable or agitated.
- **Types of Boundaries:** Boundaries can be emotional (preserving your emotional well-being), physical (your personal space and physical touch), and time-related (how you use your time).

2. Self-Awareness

- **Identify Needs:** Reflect on what you need to be respected, protected, and comfortable in your interactions.
- **Prior experiences:** Consider how prior experiences have affected your current boundary demands.

3. Clear Communication

- **Explicitly State Boundaries:** Communicate your boundaries plainly and directly to others. Be aggressive but respectful in your speech.
- **Avoid Apologies:** Setting a boundary is a healthy practice. There's no need to feel bad about taking care of yourself.

4. Consistency

- **Enforce Boundaries:** Once you've set a barrier, it's crucial to continually uphold it. Inconsistency can lead to confusion and disrespect.

- **Be Prepared for Pushback:** Not everyone will respond well to your boundaries, but it's crucial to remain firm.

5. Dealing with Boundary Violations

- **Address Violations Immediately:** If someone crosses a boundary, address it directly and swiftly.
- **Reinforce the Boundary:** Remind them of your boundary and the necessity of respecting it.

6. Setting Boundaries in Relationships

- **Mutual Respect:** In any relationship, limits should be set with mutual respect and understanding.
- **Negotiation:** Be open to discussing and negotiating limits in relationships, ensuring they work for everyone involved.

7. Professional Boundaries

- **Work-Life Balance:** Set limits to preserve a good work-life balance, such as specified work hours and personal time.
- **Professional Interactions:** Maintain professional boundaries in the workplace to maintain a respectful and productive atmosphere.

8. Personal Boundaries for Self-Care

- **Saying No:** Feel empowered to say no to requests or expectations that are beyond your capacity or comfort zone.
- **Self-Care Time:** Set aside time for self-care activities and ensure this time is respected and undisturbed.

9. Respect Others' Boundaries

- **Understanding and Respect:** Just as you set your boundaries, be understanding and respectful of the boundaries set by others.

- **Adapting to Boundaries:** Be open to changing your behavior in consideration of others' boundaries.

10. Review and Adjust Boundaries

- **Evolving Needs:** Recognize that your boundary needs may evolve and be open to adjusting them as needed.
- **Regular Check-ins:** Periodically examine your boundaries to verify they still match your needs and make adjustments if required.

Setting boundaries is a type of self-respect and a crucial strategy for maintaining successful relationships and personal well-being. It involves clear communication, consistency, and a willingness to enforce and respect these limits. By skillfully defining and managing boundaries, you may create a more balanced, respectful, and meaningful existence.

Chapter 7: Cultivating Happiness

Practices for Daily Joy

Cultivating daily joy includes integrating tiny, pleasant behaviors into your routine. These habits can enhance your mood, improve your overall well-being, and lead to a more fulfilling existence. Here's a guide on implementing habits for daily joy:

1. Gratitude

- **Gratitude Journal:** Start or end your day by writing down things you are grateful for. This exercise changes focus to the good parts of your life.
- **Expressing thanks:** Regularly show thanks to others, either vocally or by a

pleasant deed, to boost your sense of contentment.

2. Mindfulness

- **Mindful Moments:** Practice awareness throughout the day, such as during meals or while walking. Pay attention to your senses and the experience of the moment.
- **Meditation:** Incorporate a short meditation practice into your daily routine to promote mental clarity and relaxation.

3. Connection

- **Social Interaction:** Make time for meaningful connections with family, friends, or colleagues. Positive social contacts can significantly enhance your attitude.
- **Acts of Kindness:** Engage in tiny acts of kindness or volunteer activity.

Helping others can improve your sense of delight.

4. Nature and the Outdoors

- **Time in Nature:** Spend time in nature regularly, whether it's a walk in the park, gardening, or simply sitting outside. Nature has a relaxing and renewing impact.

5. Physical Activity

- **Regular Exercise:** Engage in the physical activity that you love. Exercise releases endorphins, which are natural mood boosters.
- **Stretching or Yoga:** Practice stretching or yoga to reduce physical strain and increase mental relaxation.

6. Hobbies and Interests

- **Pursue Passions:** Dedicate time to hobbies or activities that you are passionate about. Doing something you love offers natural delight.

- **Creative Expression:** Engage in creative hobbies like painting, writing, or making. Creative expression can be a fulfilling source of delight.

7. Laughter and Fun

- **Humor:** Incorporate humor into your day. Watch a funny show, read a witty book, or swap jokes with friends.
- **Playfulness:** Engage in fun activities or games. Playfulness is not just for youngsters; it may bring joy at any age.

8. Positive Affirmations

- **Affirmations:** Use positive affirmations to build a positive mindset. Repeat affirmations that resonate with your aims and aspirations.

9. Simplify Your Life

- **Declutter:** Regularly declutter your living and workstations. A tidy and ordered space can lead to a clearer mind.
- **Simplify work:** Break down work into smaller, achievable steps to decrease overwhelm and boost satisfaction.

10. Self-Care and Relaxation

- **Self-Care Rituals:** Engage in self-care rituals, such as a warm bath, reading, or listening to music.
- **Relaxation Techniques:** Practice relaxation techniques like deep breathing or progressive muscle relaxation to lessen stress.

Practices for daily joy involve simple yet effective practices that can considerably boost your quality of life. By combining gratitude, mindfulness, connection, nature, physical activity, hobbies, laughter, positive affirmations, simplification, and self-care into your daily routine, you may develop a more pleasant and full existence. Remember, the key to these activities is constancy and attention in their implementation.

Finding Happiness After Trauma

Reclaiming happiness after enduring trauma is a significant path that requires healing, self-discovery, and perseverance. This journey is unique to each individual but is anchored in specific practices and mindsets that facilitate healing and promote a return to joy and fulfillment. Here's a way to find pleasure after trauma:

1. Acknowledge and Validate Your Feelings

- **Emotional Acceptance:** Acknowledge the variety of feelings you experience as a result of trauma. It's vital to validate your sentiments, whatever they may be.
- **Seek Professional Help:** Consider therapy as a safe environment to process your feelings and work through the trauma.

2. Practice Self-Compassion

- **Kindness to Self:** Treat oneself with the same kindness and empathy you would offer a good friend.
- **Forgive Yourself:** Release any self-blame related to the trauma. Remember, healing takes time and is not a linear process.

3. Reconnect with Your Body

- **Mind-Body Practices:** Engage in activities like yoga, tai chi, or meditation, which can help you reconnect with your body and quiet your mind.
- **Physical Exercise:** Regular physical activity can enhance mood, reduce stress, and help alleviate symptoms of sadness and anxiety.

4. Develop a Supportive Network

- **Reach Out:** Connect with friends, family, or support groups who can provide emotional support and understanding.
- **Share Your Story:** When you're ready, sharing your experience can be healing and can also help others who have gone through similar events.

5. Create a Routine

- **Structure Your Day:** Establish a daily pattern that includes time for work, rest, and activities you like. Routine can create a sense of normalcy and stability.

6. Engage in Meaningful Activities

- **Pursue Interests:** Rediscover old interests or find new activities that provide you joy and a sense of achievement.

- **Volunteer Work:** Helping others can create a sense of purpose and boost feelings of self-worth.

7. Focus on the Present

- **Mindfulness:** Practice mindfulness to stay anchored in the present moment. This can help in minimizing rumination and worry about the past or future.
- **Savor minor Moments:** Learn to appreciate and savor the minor joys and triumphs in everyday life.

8. Foster Positivity

- **Good Thinking:** Challenge negative thought habits and focus on the good parts of your life.
- **Gratitude:** Keeping a gratitude notebook can help shift focus from trauma to the positive aspects of life.

9. Explore Healing Therapies

- **Trauma-Informed Therapy:** Therapies like EMDR (Eye Movement Desensitization and Reprocessing) and CBT (Cognitive Behavioral Therapy) are specifically intended for trauma recovery.
- **Creative Therapies:** Engage in creative kinds of therapy such as art therapy, music therapy, or writing, which can be therapeutic outlets.

10. Embrace New Beginnings

- **Setting Goals:** Set reasonable and achievable goals for yourself. This might offer you a sense of direction and purpose.
- **Openness to Change:** Be open to new experiences and changes. These can lead to progress and opportunity for happiness.

Finding happiness after trauma is a journey of healing, self-care, and rediscovery. It entails acknowledging and working through grief, reconnecting with oneself and others, and gradually building a life that offers fulfillment and joy. While the journey may have its problems, it is also defined by tenacity, fortitude, and the possibility of significant personal growth.

Chapter 8: Guiding the Next Generation

Breaking the Cycle of Trauma

Breaking the cycle of trauma is a vital step in preventing its replication throughout generations and in individual lives. This process involves recognizing the patterns of trauma, understanding its impact, and developing measures to heal and prevent its recurrence. Here is a way to break the cycle of trauma:

1. Recognize the Patterns

- **Understand Trauma:** Learn about the nature of trauma and its possible implications on behavior, relationships, and health.
- **Find Personal Patterns:** Reflect on your own life to find any behaviors or

patterns that may have come from past trauma.

2. Seek Professional Help

- **Therapy:** Engage in therapy with a professional versed in trauma. Therapies like Cognitive Behavioral Therapy (CBT) or Eye Movement Desensitization and Reprocessing (EMDR) can be particularly useful.
- **Support Groups:** Consider joining support groups where you may share experiences and solutions with people who are also working to break the cycle of trauma.

3. Develop Self-Awareness

- **Mindfulness and Reflection:** Practice mindfulness and self-reflection to raise your awareness of how trauma affects your thoughts and actions.

- **Journaling:** Keep a journal to monitor your feelings, triggers, and progress. This can help in understanding and regulating your responses to trauma.

4. Foster Emotional Regulation

- **Coping Strategies:** Develop healthy coping techniques for stress and emotional suffering, such as deep breathing, meditation, or exercise.
- **Emotional Intelligence:** Work on understanding and managing your emotions, and identifying the emotions of others.

5. Build Healthy Relationships

- **Communication Skills:** Learn good communication skills to express your wants and feelings effectively and to listen to others empathetically.

- **Boundary Setting:** Practice setting and keeping appropriate boundaries in your interactions.

6. Break the Silence

- **Talk About Trauma:** Openly discussing trauma and its repercussions can remove stigma and create an environment where healing is encouraged.
- **Educate Others:** Share your understanding of trauma with family, friends, or community members to raise awareness.

7. Prioritize Self-Care

- **Physical Health:** Maintain a healthy lifestyle, including frequent exercise, a balanced diet, and appropriate sleep.
- **Mental Health:** Engage in activities that improve mental well-being, such as hobbies, relaxation techniques, and spending time in nature.

8. Create a Supportive Environment

- **Positive Surroundings:** Surround yourself with helpful and understanding individuals. A good environment is vital for recovery.
- **Eliminate Harmful Influences:** Identify and withdraw yourself from situations or relationships that perpetuate the cycle of trauma.

9. Empowerment and Advocacy

- **Personal Empowerment:** Focus on your strengths and achievements. Empowerment is crucial to overcome the sense of powerlessness that trauma can cause.
- **Advocate for Change:** Get involved in advocacy or volunteer activities linked to preventing and addressing trauma.

10. Educate the Next Generation

- **Teach Coping Skills:** Educate youngsters about healthy strategies to cope with stress and emotional issues.
- **Model Healthy Behavior:** Demonstrate healthy emotional and relational behaviors to create a positive example for children and others in your community.

Breaking the cycle of trauma is a multidimensional process that requires identifying trauma, getting treatment, gaining emotional intelligence, establishing healthy relationships, and creating supportive settings. It is a path of self-discovery, healing, and empowerment that not only benefits the individual but may also have a tremendous impact on families and communities. By actively striving to interrupt the pattern, it is possible to prepare the way for a healthier, more resilient future.

Being a Source of Strength for Children

Being a source of strength for children means providing a stable, supportive atmosphere that fosters their well-being and development. It's about being a positive role model, offering support and direction, and establishing a safe atmosphere where they may develop. Here's how to be a source of strength for children:

1. Provide Unconditional Love and Support

- **Emotional Availability:** Be emotionally available to youngsters. Listen to them, acknowledge their sentiments, and show that you care.
- **Consistency:** Provide consistent care and attention. Consistency in your conduct and responses helps youngsters feel comfortable.

2. Foster Open Communication

- **Encourage Expression:** Encourage children to express their views and feelings. Create an environment where kids feel secure to share without fear of judgment.
- **Active Listening:** Practice active listening. Show interest in what they say and reply empathetically.

3. Model Positive Behavior

- **Lead by Example:** Children learn by observing. Exhibit behaviors you like kids to mimic, such as kindness, patience, and resilience.
- **Healthy Coping Strategies:** Demonstrate healthy ways to manage stress and emotions.

4. Encourage Independence and Self-Efficacy

- **Promote Problem-Solving:** Encourage youngsters to solve problems on their own, providing help when appropriate.

- **Celebrate Efforts:** Acknowledge their efforts and achievements, not just the outcomes, to build their sense of self-efficacy.

5. Establish a Safe and Secure Environment

- **Physical Safety:** Ensure a safe physical environment for children to play and explore.
- **Emotional Safety:** Create an atmosphere where children feel emotionally protected and understood.

6. Educate Them About Boundaries

- **Teach Personal Boundaries:** Educate children about personal boundaries and respect for others' boundaries.
- **Lead by Respecting Their Boundaries:** Respect children's

boundaries in terms of their bodies, privacy, and personal space.

7. Promote Resilience

- **Support in Challenges:** Support children in overcoming challenges, offering advice but enabling them to experience manageable degrees of difficulty.
- **Resilience qualities:** Teach qualities like adaptability, optimism, and the ability to bounce back from adversity.

8. Nurture Their Interests and Talents

- **Encourage Exploration:** Encourage youngsters to explore their interests and develop their talents.
- **Provide Resources:** Provide the resources and opportunities they need to follow their passions.

9. Build Positive Relationships

- **Social Skills:** Teach and model positive social skills, like cooperation, sharing, and empathy.
- **Community Involvement:** Involve children in community activities to build a sense of belonging and connection.

10. Promote Mental and Physical Health

- **Healthy Lifestyle:** Encourage a healthy lifestyle, including nutritious nutrition, physical activity, and proper sleep.
- **Mental Health Awareness:** Be aware of and handle any mental health difficulties. Teach kids that it's okay to seek help.

Being a source of strength for children is about much more than providing for their fundamental necessities. It's about supporting their emotional and psychological well-being, giving kids essential life skills, and modeling positive conduct. Through love, support, and direction, you may help children develop into resilient, confident, and well-rounded persons.

Chapter 9: Continuing the Journey

Lifelong Learning and Growth

Lifelong learning and growth constitute a continual journey of personal development, marked by a constant quest for information, skills, and self-improvement. This approach not only benefits personal and professional life but also helps overall well-being and contentment. Here are fundamental beliefs and strategies to support lifelong learning and growth:

1. Cultivate a Growth Mindset

- **Embrace Challenges:** View challenges as opportunities for progress rather than impediments.
- **Learn from Failure:** Understand that failure is a part of the learning process

and an opportunity to gather useful insights.

2. Stay Curious

- **Explore New Interests:** Regularly explore new subjects or hobbies to extend your horizons.
- **Ask Questions:** Cultivate a habit of inquiry, asking questions to expand your grasp of many topics.

3. Continuous Skill Development

- **Professional Skills:** Continuously update and enhance your professional skills to be relevant in your field.
- **Personal talents:** Develop personal talents, such as communication, time management, or creative thinking, that boost your total capabilities.

4. Engage in Lifelong Education

- **Formal Education:** Consider possibilities for formal education, such as classes, workshops, or degrees, that correspond with your interests or job ambitions.
- **Informal Learning:** Engage in informal learning through reading, online resources, podcasts, webinars, etc.

5. Reflect and Evaluate

- **Self-Reflection:** Regularly reflect on your experiences, learning, and personal progress.
- **Set and Review Goals:** Set personal and professional goals and frequently review and revise them as appropriate.

6. Embrace Diversity of Thought

- **Seek Diverse Perspectives:** Interact with people from different backgrounds and opinions to develop a larger perspective.

- **Open-Mindedness:** Be open to new ideas and ways of thinking, especially if they challenge your present beliefs.

7. Share Knowledge and Experiences

- **Teaching and Mentoring:** Share your knowledge and experiences with others by teaching, mentoring, or coaching.
- **Community Involvement:** Participate in community activities where you can learn from and contribute to the collective knowledge.

8. Balance and Well-Being

- **Work-Life Balance:** Maintain a balance between your career development and personal life.

- **Well-Being:** Prioritize your physical, mental, and emotional well-being as part of your growth journey.

9. Stay Adaptable and Flexible

- **Adaptability:** Be adaptive in the face of change and willing to shift your approaches and strategies.
- **Resilience:** Develop resilience to bounce back from setbacks and continue your learning path.

10. Continuous Improvement

- **Feedback and Evaluation:** Seek and use feedback for continual improvement.
- **Kaizen Approach:** Adopt the philosophy of 'Kaizen,' or continuous improvement, applying tiny, consistent adjustments for long-term success.

Lifelong learning and growth are about keeping a proactive commitment to personal and professional development. It entails having a growth attitude, keeping curious, regularly updating skills, and engaging in multiple types of learning. By embracing this adventure, you open yourself to a world of unlimited possibilities and prospects for fulfillment and achievement.

Staying Committed to Personal Healing

Staying devoted to personal healing is a critical element of overcoming previous trauma, managing mental health difficulties, and developing overall well-being. This commitment involves persistence, patience, and a range of tactics to maintain development and minimize setbacks. Here are crucial behaviors to assist stay dedicated to your healing journey:

1. Set Clear, Achievable Goals

- **Define Healing Objectives:** Identify what personal healing means to you and make clear, achievable goals relating to your emotional, mental, and physical health.
- **Small, Measurable Steps:** Break down these goals into smaller, manageable steps to track progress and keep motivated.

2. Develop a Supportive Network

- **Seek Support:** Build a network of support that may include friends, family, therapists, or support groups.
- **Community Engagement:** Engage in communities, either in-person or online, where you can share experiences and seek support from people with similar journeys.

3. Regular Self-Reflection

- **Journaling:** Keep a journal to reflect on your feelings, struggles, and achievements. Journaling might provide insights into your healing process.
- **Mindfulness Practices:** Engage in mindfulness or meditation to stay connected with your present experiences and sensations.

4. Embrace Self-Compassion
- **Be Kind to Yourself:** Practice self-compassion. Recognize that recovery

is a journey with ups and downs, and be gentle with yourself through the process.

- **Forgive Yourself:** Let go of self-blame and recognize that healing takes time.

5. Maintain Consistent Routines

- **Routine for Stability:** Establish and maintain routines that provide stability and a sense of normalcy.

- **Incorporate Healing Practices:** Include activities and practices in your daily routine that contribute to your healing, such as exercise, reading, or therapy sessions.

6. Stay Educated and Informed

- **Learn about Healing:** Educate yourself on diverse aspects of healing, including psychological theories, self-help practices, and personal tales of healing.

- **Stay Updated:** Keep up with new studies or treatments that might improve your recovery process.

7. Practice Healthy Living

- **Physical Health:** Take care of your physical health with regular exercise, a balanced diet, and appropriate sleep.
- **Avoid Harmful Substances:** Avoid or restrict substances that can negatively affect your mental health, such as alcohol or drugs.

8. Seek Professional Help When Needed

- **Therapy:** Regularly attend therapy sessions and be open with your therapist about your issues and progress.
- **Medical Advice:** Seek medical advice for any physical symptoms or mental health issues.

9. Celebrate Progress

- **Acknowledge Achievements:** Celebrate your achievements, no matter how minor. Recognizing progress is vital for retaining motivation.
- **Share Your Successes:** Share your progress with your support network to reinforce positive changes.

10. Adapt and Adjust

- **Flexibility:** Be willing to alter your healing tactics as your needs and circumstances change.
- **Openness to Change:** Embrace changes in your healing path as chances for development and learning.

Staying devoted to personal healing is an ongoing and evolving process. It takes setting reasonable goals, building a supporting network, practicing self-compassion, keeping healthy routines, staying educated, and recognizing accomplishments. Remember, healing is not linear and may involve setbacks, but with determination and the correct tactics, it is possible to advance toward a healthier and more rewarding life.

Conclusion

As we draw this book, "Parental Healing: Overcoming Childhood Trauma and Fostering Inner Strength," to a close, it's vital to reflect on the essential facts we've examined. The journey of healing from childhood trauma is not a path walked in isolation nor one that follows a straight line. It is a voyage of deep inner discovery, resilience, and transformation.

Understanding the Nature of Trauma

Our exploration begins with understanding the nature of childhood trauma. We discovered that trauma takes various forms and its impact is powerful and far-reaching. It forms our emotional environment, influences our behavior, and leaves impressions on our physical health. Recognizing and accepting the depth of this influence is the first step toward recovery.

The Courage to Seek Help

Seeking professional help is a courageous and crucial step in the healing journey. It's a step that demands one to confront sorrow and vulnerability head-on, but it's also a step that leads to tremendous growth and insight. Therapy, support groups, and other professional interventions provide the tools and assistance needed to traverse the complexity of healing.

Embracing Vulnerability and Building Resilience

Throughout the book, we stress the power of vulnerability. Opening up about our deepest hurts is not a sign of weakness, but rather, a bold act that paves the door for genuine healing. By embracing our vulnerabilities, we also learn to build resilience. We build the strength to tackle life's obstacles and emerge stronger.

The Power of Relationships in Healing

We dug into the vital importance of connections in the healing process. Healing is not a path that one pursues in solitude. The support, understanding, and love from others are crucial to our healing. Learning to create and maintain good relationships, including setting appropriate boundaries, are crucial skills that encourage not only our well-being but also the well-being of those around us.

Cultivating Happiness and Inner Strength

One of the most significant discoveries on this journey is the awareness that, despite prior pain, happiness and inner strength are attainable. We explored skills like gratitude, mindfulness, and self-care that can promote joy in our daily lives. We learned that happiness is not a faraway dream, but a present possibility, fostered via active activities and a good mindset.

Breaking the Cycle and Guiding the Next Generation

A crucial element of recovering from childhood trauma is the commitment to break the cycle. By healing ourselves, we are in a better position to be a source of strength, not just for ourselves, but for others, especially children. We have the potential to rewrite the narrative for the next generation, guiding them with the lessons acquired from our experiences.

The Journey Continues

It's crucial to understand that the road to healing is continuing. There will be setbacks and hurdles, but each step, no matter how tiny, is a stride towards a happier, more satisfied life. The road to healing is as much about rediscovering joy and beauty in life as it is about addressing and overcoming old pain.

A Message of Hope and Empowerment

This book offers a message of optimism and empowerment. It's a monument to the human spirit's ability to overcome misfortune and find strength in vulnerability. The tales recounted, the tactics discussed, and the insights presented are intended to light a way for people who desire to heal from their childhood trauma.

As you close this book, view it not as an end but as a new beginning on your path. Take the lessons acquired, the tactics examined, and the insights obtained, and apply them to your life. Remember, recovery is a personal path, unique to each individual. Be patient with yourself, be kind, and most importantly, be open to the boundless possibilities that healing brings.

In Gratitude and Hope

In closing, I extend my deepest thanks to you, the reader, for going on this trip with me. Your desire to explore the depths of healing from childhood trauma is a brave and major step. It is my honest goal that this book has offered you with understanding, comfort, and a roadmap toward a life of healing, happiness, and inner strength.

May you find serenity on your journey, joy in your accomplishments, and strength in your continued progress. The road to healing is littered with hardships, but it's also packed with hope, love, and the promise of a brighter, more meaningful future. Keep moving forward, one step at a time, and realize that you are not alone on this path.